ICE HOCKEY LEGENDS

Wayne Gretzky

Brett Hull

Jaromir Jagr

Mario Lemieux

Eric Lindros

Mark Messier

CHELSEA HOUSE PUBLISHERS

ICE HOCKEY LEGENDS

MARK MESSIER

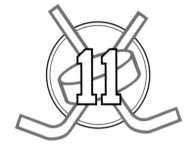

Barry Wilner

CHELSEA HOUSE PUBLISHERS
Philadelphia

Produced by Daniel Bial and Associates
New York, New York

Picture research by Alan Gottlieb
Cover illustration by Earl Parker

First Printing

1 3 5 7 9 8 6 4 2

Library of Congress Cataloging-in-Publication Data

Wilner, Barry.
        Mark Messier / by Barry Wilner.
            p.   cm. — (Ice hockey legends)
        Includes bibliographical references (p.   ) and index.
        Summary: An inside account of the life of the New York Rangers
    hockey star.
        ISBN 0-7910-4559-5
        1. Messier, Mark, 1961–   — Juvenile literature. 2. Hockey
    players — Canada — Biography — Juvenile literature.   [1. Messier,
    Mark, 1961 –   . 2. Hockey players.] I. Title. II. Series.
    GV848.5.M47W55   1997
    796.962'092—dc21
    [B]
                                                            97-27364
                                                                CIP
                                                                 AC

CONTENTS

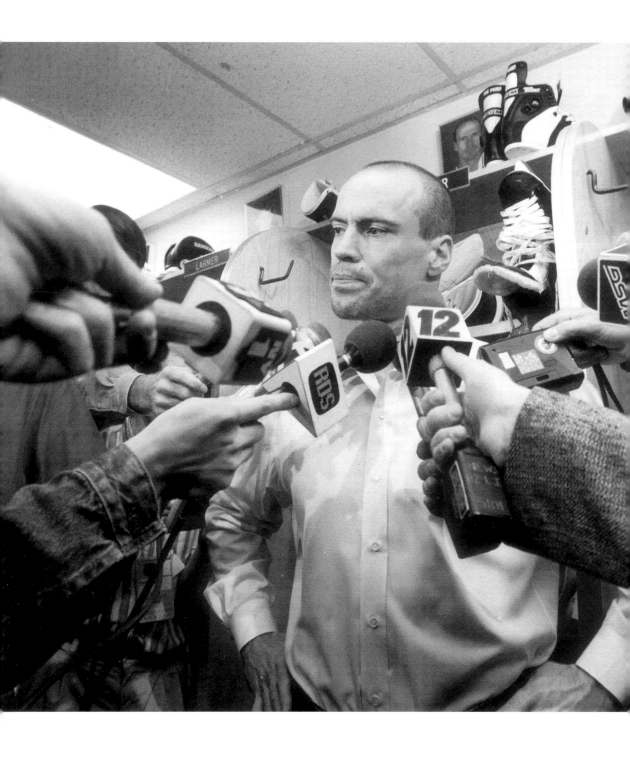

MESSIER'S GREATEST GAME

Athletes don't usually like to make guarantees. Oh, sure, Muhammad Ali predicted victories in the boxing ring, even naming the round his opponent would fall. And Joe Namath said it straight out before the 1969 Super Bowl, then led the New York Jets to one of the biggest upsets in sports history.

Mark Messier made a guarantee also, to hockey fans in the spring of 1994. And, as the great ones do, Messier delivered.

The Rangers had the best record in the National Hockey League (NHL) in the 1993-94 season, yet they trailed the New Jersey Devils—who had the second-best mark during the season—3-2 in the Eastern Conference finals.

Game 6 was set for the Byrne Arena in New Jersey. The Devils had plenty of momentum after winning the fourth and fifth games of the intense series between teams whose homes sit 10 miles apart.

In 1994, Mark Messier boldly predicted a win for his New York Rangers.

The Rangers brought Messier to New York to lead them to a Stanley Cup championship—which they had not won in 54 years. "Mess" was the most successful hockey player in recent memory. He won four Cups when Wayne Gretzky was the centerpiece of the Edmonton Oilers, and he won another in 1990, two years after Gretzky was traded to Los Angeles.

Messier (left) is pumped after Stephane Matteau scored the winning goal in double over-time during the 1994 matchups between the Rangers and Devils.

So he knew what it takes to be a champ. And he showed he was not afraid of putting his reputation on the line. "We think we are going to go in there and win Game 6," Messier said. "We've done it all year. We've responded all year when we have had to. We know we are going to go in there and win Game 6 and bring it back to the Garden."

So he guaranteed Game 6. Little did he know he'd have to have the greatest game of his career to make that guarantee come true.

The Devils opened a 2-0 lead on goals by Scott Niedermayer and Claude Lemieux, and goaltender Martin Brodeur stopped several good chances by New York.

The crowd at the Meadowlands was in a mood for celebration, certain that the defensively sound

Devils would protect such a lead. Several fans could be heard warming up their derisive chants of "1940, 1940," the last time the Rangers had won the NHL title.

Alexei Kovalev, the promising young left wing, had struggled since Devils forward Bernie Nicholls cross-checked him in the neck in Game 3. But it was he who got the Rangers on track. With 1.41 to go in the second period, he took a drop pass from Messier and beat Brodeur from the right wing after first faking a shot.

"I think that shook them up a little bit and it gave us a lot of confidence," Messier said.

Still, the Rangers were down 2-1 entering the third period. The Rangers had not had success in come-from-behind victories; three times they had entered the third period with a deficit during these playoffs, and they had gone on to lose all of those games. Meanwhile, the Devils were 8-1 in playoff games when they took a lead into the last period.

In the dressing room, the Rangers' thoughts were simple: Go out and get the next goal. Then take it from there.

"I remember how loud the crowd was when we came out for the third period," Steve Larmer recalled. "And I looked at Mark and he had this look on his face like he had blocked it all out. It was a look of pure determination, like he was going to make this thing happen and turn out right, no matter what anyone else thought or did."

Just 2:48 into the third period, Messier turned his determination into results, tying the score 2-2.

Messier put a backhander past Brodeur and raised both arms skyward. His teammates on the ice mobbed him, and the air seemed to go out of the building the way it does when you skate over a balloon and make it pop.

But Messier wasn't through. "Once we tied it, we really started coming on," he said. "We were more relaxed, in a good kind of way, because we felt comfortable."

With 12:12 gone in the period, Messier poked a rebound past Brodeur after Kovalev's shot bounced off Brodeur—even though Nicholls was all over Messier. For just a moment after the puck went into the net, it seemed as if number 11 was the only one on the ice. All eyes were on him as he once again thrust his arms in the air, this time for a go-ahead goal.

There would be more.

To finish off his remarkable evening, especially the third period in which he lifted an entire team—indeed, an entire city that had known nothing but heartbreak from the Rangers for more than half a century—on his strong shoulders, Messier scored into an empty net with 1:45 left.

"He took it in his own hands and showed the resolve he talked about before the game," Rangers coach Mike Keenan said. "I don't have to say much, for his actions spoke as many words as I could think of. That has to rank up there with the best I've seen."

While Messier admitted the importance of his role in tying the series—the Rangers would win it dramatically in double overtime in Game 7—he refused to credit himself or his guarantee with being the deciding factor. "No one man wins the hockey game, or any championship, or anything in a team sport," Messier said.

Maybe not. But the other Rangers knew who provided the fire with which they burned New

New Jersey goalie Martin Brodeur and defenseman Bernie Nicholls could not stop Messier from scoring the winning goal in Game 6 of their playoff series.

Jersey. "He'll go down in history as one of the greatest to play the game," teammate Ed Olczyk said. "He's won MVPs, games by himself. That's why Mess is a winner. You can only learn from that."

The Devils learned just how magnificent Messier can be. "He leads and they follow," said Nicholls, whom the Rangers had traded to Edmonton to get Messier in the first place. "Your best player can't say that we have to win tonight's game, he's got to guarantee it. He went out and proved he was going to do it and they followed. That's why, in my opinion, he is the best money player in the game.

"He's the best clutch player," Nicholls continued. "I know Gretz and Mario Lemieux get a lot of credit, but when the chips are down and there is a big game to be won, there is nobody better."

EDMONTON: THE EARLY YEARS

Mark was born on January 18, 1961, and grew up in Edmonton, Alberta. Like most Canadian boys, hockey was his favorite sport. Along with his brother Paul, he took to the ice at a young age, and was lucky to have his father, Doug, as his teacher and coach. Doug Messier believed in strict rules, but he also was fair. If a player worked hard and was dedicated to the team, he got playing time.

In 1975, Doug coached the Spruce Grove Mets to the Centennial Cup, the Canadian national junior championship. Two years later, the team moved to St. Albert, a suburb of Edmonton, and became the Saints. The star player was Doug's son, Mark.

"I knew him when he was playing midget hockey in Edmonton," said Larry Mitchell, the publicist for the Saints in those days. "I remember his dad talking about him before he moved to

Messier was only 20 years old when he started playing for the Edmonton Oilers. Here he goes all out to try to get the puck away from Ranger captain Barry Beck.

13

juniors. Even then, he was a dominant player. A year out of midgets, he took charge on the ice. There was no question who was in charge with the Saints."

"Mark had basically the same style as his father, a tough guy and a leader," said Charles Lavallee, the trainer for the Saints and a friend of Mark's when they were teenagers. "When he was 17, he acted like a 20-year-old; he would look after 18- and 19-year-old players better than 20-year-olds did. Mark was just meant to be a leader."

He led the Mets scoring in the 1976-77 season with 66 points (27 goals, 39 assists). The next year, with the Saints, he had 25 goals and 74 points. In March 1978, the Saints opened a new arena in St. Albert. Messier needed only 27 seconds to score the first goal in Akinsdale Arena.

"He's a very intense individual when he wants things," said Lavallee. "He gets that look in his eyes. He even had the look then; it was even worse. I always remember times when stuff was going on on the ice and he wanted to get after the tough guy on the other team. He got the Mike Tyson look, then he went after the guy and took care of him."

One time, he challenged everybody on the Port Saskatchewan team to fight him before a playoff game. Nobody would. Throughout the game, which St. Albert won, none of the Saints players were checked hard. Mark had taken the nerve away from the opponent.

When the Saints' season ended, Mark went to play for Portland (Oregon) of the Western Hockey League in the playoffs and had four goals.

That was it for juniors. Mark was ready for a bigger challenge. It came in the form of the World

Hockey Association, which was competing against the older NHL and was willing to sign players under the age of 18.

The Indianapolis Racers signed Messier to replace a player they had just sold to the Edmonton Oilers. They were running short of money, and knew they wouldn't be able to hold on to Wayne Gretzky for long.

Mark lasted only five games in Indianapolis, then was traded to Cincinnati. He had only one goal and 10 assists in 47 games. But he was learning.

"I was young and away from home for the first time, and I had to adjust to playing against guys much older than me," he said. "I had to realize I wasn't a kid anymore."

At the end of the season, the WHA folded. Four teams were admitted into the NHL, but Cincinnati was not one of them. Messier, without a contract, was free to sign with any team he wanted . . . and he chose his hometown Edmonton Oilers.

Their first season in the NHL was nothing special for the Oilers. Gretzky, of course, was an immediate star and was voted the league's MVP. But Messier had only 33 points and spent four games in the minor leagues.

Few of the other young players had big years. Instead, they tried to learn what life in the NHL was like, and they found out it was hard. Edmonton sneaked into the playoffs as the 16th and last team. They managed to take two games against Philadelphia, which had the league's best record, into overtime, before being swept in the first-round series.

The next season wasn't much better. The Oilers won only 29 games, one more than the year before. But they made major progress in the play-offs, upsetting the Montreal Canadiens in a three-game sweep that stunned all of Canada. "We were growing together as a team, getting to know one another on and off the ice," Gretzky said. "We knew we were getting closer to the top, but the record didn't show it."

The Islanders eliminated Edmonton in six games, but the Oilers had gotten a taste of post-season success. They were anxious for more.

At some point in the story of all great teams and all great players, things mesh. Problems disappear. What you once struggled to do becomes easy. And you win. For the Oilers, that started happening in the 1981-82 season. Led by Gretzky, who had the greatest year in hockey history with 92 goals and 212 points, Edmonton went from 29 to 48 wins, from 74 points to 111, from 14th place overall to second.

Messier, who had 23 goals and 63 points the year before, jumped to 50 goals and 88 points. At the age of 21, he became a true star, the best left wing in hockey. "I think Mark really made himself known to everyone that year," said teammate Kevin Lowe. "It wasn't, 'Who is Messier' anymore. It was 'Watch out for Messier.'"

However, the Oilers crashed in the playoffs. There was no panic after a comical 10-8 loss to Los Angeles in the first game of the opening round. All was calm when a 3-2 victory followed, even though it took overtime to get it.

Not even when the Kings took Game 3, also in overtime, were the Oilers getting uptight. Worried, yes. Panicking, no. Another 3-2 win sent the series back to Edmonton, where Messier was sure who would win.

"We just have a better team," he said. "I really believe that."

The Kings, though, were annoyed that the Oilers celebrated a bit too loudly, even saying some Edmonton players taunted them after Oilers goals. They felt everyone—including the Oilers—had written them off.

"There's a lot at stake for us here, too," said Charlie Simmer, the Kings' star left wing. "We didn't come here just to be the Oilers' victims. We came here to win."

Shockingly, they did. It wasn't close, either: Kings 7, Oilers 4.

As the fans silently emptied out of Northlands Coliseum, the players sat in their locker room, stunned. Some cried. Some threw equipment. None of them could understand how they could

Goalie Billy Smith of the New York Islanders protests, but Mark Messier has just scored during the 1983 Stanley Cup finals. Behind the net, Ken Morrow tries to keep Messier's teammate, Lee Fogolin, away from any rebounds.

lose to a weaker opponent. "This is going to hurt for a long time," Messier said. "Hopefully, it will make us stronger."

The Oilers learned their lesson. They'd been forced to grow up quickly after their inexcusable loss to the Kings.

The 1982-83 season brought more of the same firepower. They won the Smythe Division again, finishing third in the overall standings. Messier and Gretzky made the NHL All-Star Team, with Mark going over the 100-point plateau (48 goals, 58 assists, 106 points) for the first time. They scored 424 goals, seven more than in the record-setting previous season.

When the playoffs rolled around, the Oilers were certain they were ready for anything. Winnipeg fell in three straight in the opening round, then Calgary went down in five and Chicago in four. The Oilers had gone deeper into the playoffs than ever. "We felt we should have been here last year," Messier said. "We're definitely playing our best hockey."

They would need it against the Islanders, who'd struggled to get to the finals for the fourth straight year. New York won the first three times it had gotten this far, but Edmonton was actually favored in this series, which began at Northlands Coliseum.

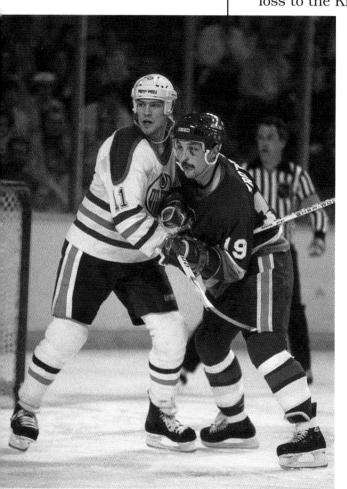

Messier outplayed Islanders star Bryan Trottier, and the Oilers broke New York's streak and started their own Stanley Cup–winning streak in 1984.

"We're the champions until somebody beats us," said Islanders goalie Billy Smith, whose crit-

icism of the Oilers and their fans made him Pub-
lic Enemy number one in Edmonton. One news-
paper ran a front-page picture of Smith inside
a bull's-eye. Smith just laughed at the outrage
and stopped everything sent his way in a 2-0
victory in Game 1.

That set the tone for the series. The Islanders
then blew away the Oilers in four games, allow-
ing them to brag about being the best in hockey history, while leaving Messier muttering to
himself.

"Six goals in four games," said Messier, who
played with a separated shoulder. "It's impossi-
ble to believe they shut us off like that.

"It seemed we would come into the dressing
room after every period in every game and say,
'Hey, we had our chances. Let's get a few goals
and bury them.' We kept saying it right to the
end. It never happened."

Maybe it would happen the next year, when
the teams would meet again. But this time, there
was a difference: the Oilers had learned to play
better defense.

It didn't show much in the regular season,
when Edmonton had the league's best record
(57-18-5, a franchise mark that still stands) and
scored an incredible 446 goals. Messier had
switched to center in February—when coach
Glen Sather decided the team needed a stronger
force in the middle when Gretzky was off the
ice—and still scored 101 points.

It wasn't clear early in the playoffs, when the
Oilers staged shootouts with Winnipeg and Calgary. They outscored the Jets 18-7 in a three-
game sweep, then were stretched to seven games
to beat the Flames. Only one game in that series
had fewer than seven goals.

When the Oilers swept away Minnesota in the semifinals, outscoring the North Stars 22-10 in four games, it was more because the Oilers always had the puck than because they held the opponent in check.

Then came the finals, with Game 1 on Long Island. The Islanders were after a record-tying fifth straight Stanley Cup. The Oilers were after revenge.

"We think we can play with them, but until we beat them in a playoff game, well, we haven't proven anything, have we?" Messier said.

The opener was exactly the kind of game the Islanders wanted and the Oilers usually failed at. It featured tight checking, great goaltending, and pressure, pressure, pressure.

This time, it was the Islanders who broke. Kevin McClelland, a third-string center, got the only goal in a 1-0 Oilers victory.

"You have no idea what this win means," said Messier, who checked Islanders star Bryan Trottier right out of the game. "It shows we can play any style and win, including their style."

Although the Islanders came back to win Game 2 easily, the Oilers were pumped up when they went home

A jubilant Messier celebrates after receiving the Conn Smythe trophy, which honors the most valuable player of the Stanley Cup finals.

for the next three games. They never let up.

First came a 7-2 romp. Then another 7-2 rout.
Then a 5-2 clincher.

Messier was the leader, scoring eight goals and
18 assists in the playoffs, playing strong defense,
winning faceoffs, and earning the Conn Smythe
Trophy as MVP.

"It's just a kicker on top of it all," he said of
the MVP award. "The thought of winning the
Conn Smythe never once entered my mind. I
don't think I worked harder than 20 other guys
on this team."

Others knew Messier had been the difference.
"He deserved it hands down," Paul Coffey said.
"There was no other choice."

"Last year, we didn't have a healthy Mark
Messier and it hurt," Sather added. "This year,
you saw what he can do. He proved he's a great
player."

He proved he's a champion, too. So when it
was his turn to carry the Stanley Cup, Messier
shook with excitement.

"I've rehearsed this the last two months," he
said. "Actually, the last five years, since I turned
pro. But especially the last two months. Every
night before I went to bed, I would think, 'What
do you do if you win? How do you carry the Cup
around the ice?'"

When the time came, he knew.

EDMONTON: BUILDING THE DYNASTY

Having finally won a Stanley Cup, everyone knew what was next: another championship. "There was no question in our minds that we were the best team in hockey," Messier said. "But you have to prove it again every year."

In 1984-85, proving anything came hard for Messier. He played in only 55 games. After injuring his left knee in Winnipeg on November 4, he was sidelined for 15 games. He missed another 10 when he was suspended for breaking the cheekbone of Calgary's Jamie Macoun with a punch.

Messier said he hit Macoun in return for a check the Calgary player had put on him earlier in the game. "I snapped," said Messier. "But if I don't get even for a thing like that, I have a short career. What he did was a deliberate attempt to injure. I don't regret anything at all."

Wayne Gretzky (right) may be the greatest hockey player of all time. But he needed excellent teammates to help him shine and none helped more than his friend Mark Messier.

Another key to the Oilers' success was goalie Grant Fuhr. Here he turns away the attempts of Chicago Blackhawk Jack O'Callahan to score during the 1985 playoffs. Also helping out are Oilers Dave Hunter (12) and Kevin Lowe (4).

Again at the top of the Campbell Conference, the Oilers finished the year 49-20-11. That was a little less impressive than the previous season's record, but still good. And Messier managed 54 points in those 55 games.

The playoffs began almost as if they'd never ended for the Oilers, who swept Los Angeles in the first round and Winnipeg in the second. "We feel like we're unstoppable, as long as we keep playing this way, working this way," Messier said. "We have the players, the experience and the confidence to win."

Things got tougher in the semifinals against Chicago, which pushed the Oilers to six games. But when Jari Kurri scored four times in an 8-2 rout, Edmonton moved into its third straight Stanley Cup final.

The Philadelphia Flyers didn't put up much of a challenge after winning Game 1 at home. Edmonton took the next four, winning tight-checking games and wide-open contests. "We feel we can win any game we're in, regardless of what the score is," said Messier.

Mark finished with 25 points in 18 postseason games, another strong showing. Wayne Gretzky was the playoff MVP, however, which was just fine with Messier. During the locker room celebration of their second straight Cup, Messier held up the Conn Smythe Trophy and said to everyone, "Last year, I got this. Now, Wayne. Who's next?"

To be considered among the greatest teams of all time, the Oilers felt they had to win a third straight title. The Islanders won four in a row and the Montreal Canadiens did the same thing from 1976-79. From 1956-60, the Canadiens won five years in a row—the only team in an international league of any sport ever to win five straight championships.

The Oilers played all season as if they were up to the challenge, too, going 56-17-7, the best record in the league and just one win fewer than in their first Cup season. Messier missed 17 games after badly bruising his left foot when hit by a shot by Bernie Nicholls. He still wound up with 35 goals and 84 points and had one of his best all-around seasons.

After sweeping Vancouver in the opening round, the Oilers prepared for the "Battle of

Alberta" with Calgary. "We know that nobody likes to beat Calgary more than Edmonton and nobody likes to beat Edmonton more than Calgary," said Messier, who was aware of that his whole life, having grown up in the Edmonton area. "We had a brutal series with them two years ago. It will be brutal again."

The Flames hadn't won in Edmonton in the past five regular seasons. Surprise: they won the opener of the series, 4-1. "If we would have come out of that game with a win it would have been a crime," said Edmonton defenseman Paul Coffey. "They played a great, great hockey game."

The Flames also played well in Game 2, but Glenn Anderson's overtime goal saved the Oilers from being down two games heading to Calgary. Calgary had tied it in the final minute of the third period before Anderson won it 6-5.

In Game 3, Calgary, which had finished 30 points behind Edmonton in the Smythe Division, eked out a 3-2 victory. "They're working as hard as any team we've ever played against," Messier said. "Maybe we can work harder. We know we can play better."

The Oilers played much better in the fourth game, bombing goalie Mike Vernon in a 7-4 win. Vernon, the star of the first three games, was benched in the third period of Game 4. But he bounced back with a great performance in the fifth game, which was the Flames' second 4-1 win at the Oilers' home. Edmonton's stars, from Messier to Gretzky to Kurri to Coffey to Anderson, were all silent. "I don't think we ever imagined we could be in a position like this, "Messier said before Game 6. "If we're a championship team, we'll respond."

They did, winning for the second time in Calgary and forcing a seventh game. Messier's short-handed goal tied it after the Oilers fell behind 2-0, and Anderson got the winner in a 5-2 victory.

So it was back to Edmonton, where the Oilers believed they couldn't lose a third time to the Flames. But they didn't count on one of the weirdest goals in NHL history making the difference.

By 2:08 of the second period, the Flames led 2-0. Then the Oilers rallied on goals by Anderson and Messier, whose breakaway shot beat the rookie Vernon late in the second period.

The Oilers seemed ready to take control. With 5:14 gone in the third period, Oilers rookie defenseman Steve Smith had the puck behind his net. He meant to pass it ahead to a forward, but instead the puck went off the skate of goalie Grant Fuhr, who was looking up ice. And it trickled into the net. "I can never recall a goal going in like that. You never expect something like that," Fuhr said.

It was too much for the Oilers to overcome. Calgary held on to win the series and end Edmonton's hopes of a third straight Cup.

"It's the worst feeling I've ever had in my life," Smith said, his eyes still red from crying as he

One of Messier's greatest strengths is killing off penalties while the opposing team has a man advantage. Here he scores a short-handed goal against Ron Hextall of the Philadelphia Flyers during the 1987 playoffs.

sat in the Oilers' silent dressing room. "I was just trying to make a pass out front to two guys circling. It was a human error. I got good wood on it, it just didn't go in the direction I wanted."

The Oilers felt haunted throughout the 1986–87 season by their failure against Calgary. "We've spent this whole year trying to prove ourselves again," Messier said as the Oilers entered the playoffs off a 50-victory season. "It's time to show we're good enough to win another Cup."

The first challenge wasn't much of a challenge as the Oilers beat the Kings in five games. Edmonton was even better in the next round, sweeping Winnipeg. But it never is that easy, and the Oilers—off an eight-day rest—lost the opener of the conference finals 3-1 to Detroit.

"That woke us up," Messier said. "We should have realized from what happened last year that anybody can beat you when you're not at your best. We know we have to be at our best every night."

For the next four games, they were just that, eliminating the Red Wings. "They have the greatest player in the world [Gretzky] and the second-greatest player in the world [Messier]," Red Wings coach Jacques Demers said. "What can you do?" There wasn't much Detroit could do with Messier, who scored four goals and physically dominated the series.

Next up were the highly physical Flyers, the Broad Street Bullies. The Oilers handled them in the 1985 finals, but these Flyers were stronger. Yet the Oilers won three of the first four games. They could have swept the series, but they blew a 3-0 lead in Philadelphia in Game 3.

Heading home for the fifth game, which nearly everyone thought would be the clincher, the

Oilers claimed they wouldn't get too confident, wouldn't look ahead and think about celebrating. That's what they said. But they blew 2-0 and 3-1 leads and fell in Game 5. They led 2-0 before falling in Game 6, forcing a decisive seventh contest, in Edmonton. The Oilers only had to look back a year to the Calgary series to know how dangerous that can be.

When the Flyers took a 1-0 lead, all of Edmonton must have shuddered. But Messier tied it, then Kurri and Anderson scored to clinch the third Cup. "In our minds, last year never should have happened," Messier said. "But it did, and this is the only way to make up for it."

With three titles in four years, the Oilers were one of hockey's best teams ever. One more championship, they believed, would stamp them as an equal to the recent Islanders and Canadiens who dominated the NHL.

But the road to a fourth Cup did not start well. In a contract dispute, Messier held out. He didn't report to training camp and was suspended by coach-GM Glen Sather. Messier needed a break after helping Canada win the Canada Cup. But was this the way to do it? Also, Coffey was unhappy with his contract and holding out.

Messier worked out a new contract rather quickly, but Coffey wound up being traded to Pittsburgh. It was a bad sign for the Oilers, who soon would be broken up; owner Peter Pocklington decided he couldn't afford such high-priced players. But before Pocklington destroyed a great team, the Oilers had one more championship run with most of their stars still aboard.

This time, it was Messier who was dominant, even though Gretzky would win his second playoff MVP trophy. "We couldn't handle Messier," said Winnipeg star Dale Hawerchuk after the Oilers won the opening round in five games.

"To lose four straight, there's not a lot to say except they played harder and more desperate than we did, and they had players like Gretzky and Messier, who we couldn't stop," said Calgary's Lanny McDonald after the Flames suffered a four-game sweep in the second round by Edmonton.

"They have the best players in the world," Detroit's Steve Yzerman said after losing to the Oilers in five games in the conference finals. "We tried hard and they tried hard, but their best players—guys like Gretzky and Messier and Fuhr and Kurri—are better than our best."

So it was back to a familiar place, the Stanley Cup finals. This time, the Boston Bruins were the opponent.

The Oilers won the first three games of the series and were tied 3-3 in Game 4 at Boston Garden when the lights went out. Building officials could not get them working again and the NHL postponed the game and continued the series as planned.

That meant going back to Edmonton for the

In 1988, Messier and Gretzky got to skate around again with the Stanley Cup—the fourth time in five years they had won the championship.

next game. "We think we're a pretty good team," Messier joked, "but we're not too good in the dark. And now we get a chance to carry the Cup around the ice at home."

For the fourth time in five years, the Oilers were champs. "We're one Stanley Cup away from being the greatest team ever," defenseman Kevin Lowe said after the Bruins were beaten. Lowe, of course, couldn't have known Pocklington's plans.

After the season, Pocklington traded Wayne Gretzky to Los Angeles in the biggest trade in hockey history.

"I thought Gretz would always be an Oiler," said Messier, the hurt quite clear in his voice. "I just can't believe this." Their lives, their hockey histories, had been connected almost since they were kids. And now, they were opponents.

Gretzky cried. So did Messier—and many other Oilers. The fans screamed for Pocklington to sell the team and get out of town.

"I guess you know this always can happen in sports," Messier said. "But when it does—especially when the greatest player in the history of the game gets traded—it's a shock. It really hurts."

They would spend eight years playing against each other in NHL games, teaming up only when they skated for Canada in international events. But there would always be a common bond. "We always kept track of each other and always stayed friends," Gretzky said. "Mark has been a big part of my career. Mark was always the leader of the Oilers."

Messier was named captain. But, without the Great One, the Oilers were hardly a great team. They fell from a 44-25-11 record and the championship in 1987-88 to 38-34-8 and were eliminated in the first round of the playoffs—by the Kings, led by Gretzky. "I think Wayne had an awful lot to prove," Messier said.

By the fall of 1989, few people expected the Oilers ever to contend for another Stanley Cup. Too many great players were done or on their way out as Pocklington cleared out big salaries.

A few months later, with Gretzky, Fuhr, and Coffey long gone, the Oilers opened their 1990 playoffs against Winnipeg. And quickly lost three of the first four games. "One of the things I felt when we were down 3-1 was Mark and the people who played on those four Stanley Cup winners gave the team a lot of support," said coach John Muckler, who was promoted when Sather gave up his bench duties. "We felt if we got some breaks, we have the more skilled hockey players, and we could win the series, which we did."

Yes, the Oilers still knew how to win, becoming the seventh team in NHL history to rally from a 3-1 hole. Then came Gretzky and the Kings, who had upset defending champion Calgary in the opening round.

"It's great and it's not so great," Messier said. "You love to be on the same ice with Gretz, competing against him. But, at the same time, it makes it tougher to win when he's on the other side."

This time it wasn't tough as the Oilers swept the Kings. While they didn't do it for the owner, it was he who enjoyed the four games the most. "This takes the monkey off my shoulders," Pocklington said. "I've been a pretty bad guy in Edmonton's eyes since a year ago August [when he traded Gretzky]. This certainly makes me feel happy to see the young guys come together."

They stayed together in the semifinals against Chicago, winning a six-game series, one of the toughest the Oilers ever played. For the sixth time in eight seasons, Edmonton was playing for the Cup.

"Our goal from the start has been to win the Stanley Cup," said Messier. "We had to get here to get to the Stanley Cup. We're going to relax for a day and then worry about Boston."

They didn't worry too much. Sure, they no longer had some big stars. But what they had left—Messier, Kurri, Anderson, Esa Tikkanen, Lowe, Bill Ranford, and Adam Graves—was enough to prove that "one for the thumb" was possible.

Messier had an MVP season with 47 goals, 84 assists, and 129 points. He was second in scoring to Gretzky. And he would tie for the playoffs points lead with 31. Most importantly, he would lead them past the Bruins in five games for his and the Oilers' fifth championship.

"I don't think there is anyone in our dressing room that has to prove anything to anyone," Messier said when asked if the Oilers had to prove they could win the Cup without Gretzky. "I think every one of these guys who were around for those four Stanley Cups, in their own mind feel that they had a lot to do with winning those Cups, as Wayne did."

Boston coach Mike Milbury knew that Messier made a difference in winning this Cup. "He's a great player," Milbury said. "I don't think you truly ever stop the great ones."

But you do trade them, and one year after winning a fifth Cup in Edmonton, Mark was headed to New York.

MARK JOINS THE RANGERS

Coming off the most frustrating, injury-plagued year of his career, Messier became the focus of trade talks. Rumors swirled all summer that the stingy Oilers would deal him away—along with his contract which called for him to earn $1.1 million in 1991-92. By September, Edmonton's general manager, Glen Sather, had spoken dozens of times with the Rangers' general manager, Neil Smith, about a possible trade. Oilers owner Peter Pocklington wanted Messier sent to a team that would give Pocklington lots of money in return. Mark simply wanted to go somewhere he could win a sixth Stanley Cup.

While Sather was trying to make the deal, his assistant, Bruce MacGregor—a former Rangers player—explained why New York. "In New York, he would be a marquee player, somebody they haven't had for a while. He'd be somebody to take over that position in a market competitive

After their dynasty years, the Oilers broke up. Gretzky and Fuhr left, and in 1991, Messier became a New York Ranger.

Despite his other duties, Messier still found time to play for his home team during the 1991 Canada Cup.

with a lot of other sports," MacGregor said. "That's why New York makes sense."

Messier didn't like the way the stars who brought so many championships to the Oilers were treated. "Forget it. There was no reward given back to those players," he said. "I wouldn't say those players kept the franchise alive. Edmonton is a great hockey city. The franchise will survive. But those are the players who kept the dynasty alive. If that's the way it's going to be in Edmonton, I don't want to be there."

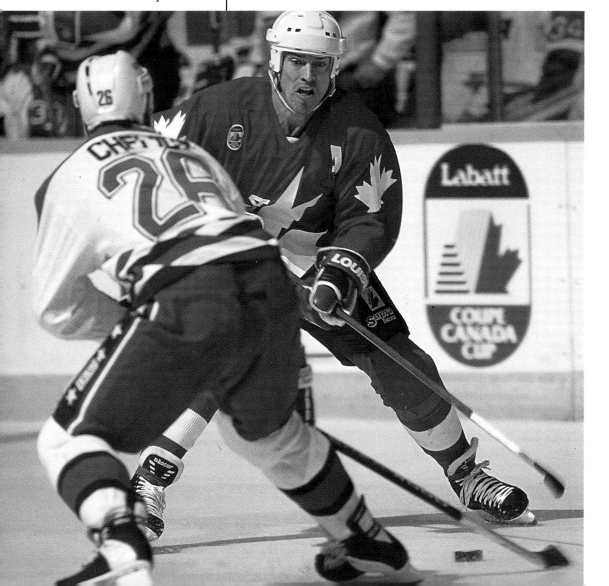

He also knew he had plenty left to offer another team. "I want to play another 10 years," Messier said just before the trade. "I think I have five more at the top of my game. I think my best years are ahead of me. People who say that when you turn 30, you start your downslide are wrong. I don't think any athlete who keeps himself in shape has to go downhill."

Reunited with Gretzky and Coffey, Mark had just helped Canada win the Canada Cup for the third straight time. He had planned to skip the international tournament, but his close friend Gretzky kept asking him to join Team Canada. "Gretzky called me three days in a row," Messier had said from his home in Hilton Head, South Carolina, where he was recovering from injuries to his knees and thumb. "He really knows how to get to a guy."

Messier scored a goal in Canada's 4-2 victory over the United States that clinched the Canada Cup. "Canada should be proud of its hockey programs. Canada hasn't lost a Cup series since '81. This is a great team," he said.

But the Oilers were no longer great. And on October 4, 1991, they sent Mark to New York.

Messier was accepted by everyone in the big city with open arms. The fans believed the Rangers had found the man who would lead them to their first Stanley Cup since 1940 and end the longest drought in pro sports. The media liked Messier's style, his honesty, and his availability. The players, well, who wouldn't want to have Mark Messier at his side—on the ice and in the locker room?

"He has an aura," said Mike Gartner, who, like Messier, began his professional career as a teenager in the WHA back in the 1970s. "He doesn't have any magic words. He just knows what to say and to do. Everyone respects what he has achieved in the game. He's just a good leader, a quality person who has been a part of winning his whole career."

Gretzky seemed just as hurt by the Messier trade as he was by his own from Edmonton to Los Angeles. "This guy wore his crest on his heart," Gretzky said. "I'm sure all of this is really weighing on Mark's mind. His family lives in Edmonton. He's from there. He grew up there."

In his first game for the team, Messier helped the Rangers end an eight-year winless streak in Montreal. His next game was his debut as a Ranger at Madison Square Garden, where he assisted on both New York goals.

He was named captain just before putting on the uniform that night. A group of former Rangers captains was introduced before the game. Then Messier received a standing ovation from the crowd of 17,542 when he came on the ice for pregame ceremonies, and he raised his stick in the air as the fans cheered. "WELCOME MARK MESSIER. WE HOPE YOU BROUGHT THE CUP," one banner read.

"I was nervous all day today," he said. "That's good for me. I play better when I'm a little nervous. My biggest worry was making sure I didn't fall in front of the other captains. Just before the game, they let me know they were going to give me the captaincy and apologized for not having enough time to talk to me about it. They asked me if I was willing to accept it, and I said I would wear it with honor."

And how would Captain Mark lead his new troops? "I think the important thing is for everyone on the team to feel the pressure," he said.

"I don't think the fear of losing is a bad thing. It's pushed me throughout my career in Edmonton, because we had a lot of pressure to win. I think we can use the same attention we get here in New York. I think we can use that to our advantage."

Messier used it. He became the third-highest-paid player in the NHL, behind Gretzky and Mario Lemieux, when he signed a five-year, $13 million contract. Then he earned that money by scoring a team-high 107 points, fifth in the NHL. He had a 15-game points streak and three hat tricks, including a four-goal game versus New Jersey.

The Rangers had the best record in the league. But the NHL players then went on strike, unhappy they did not have a contract with the league. The walkout lasted only 10 days, but it destroyed the Rangers' momentum. After eliminating New Jersey in a tiring seven-game series—Messier had two goals in the Game 7 clincher—they met defending champion Pittsburgh, led by the great Lemieux. It was a wonderful matchup: hock-

Messier was called upon to help stop Pittsburgh's best player, Mario Lemieux, during the playoffs. The Penguins, however, went on to take the Stanley Cup in both 1991 and 1992.

ey's smoothest superstar against the sport's most intense leader.

But Messier missed Game 2 with back spasms. In that game, Rangers teammate Adam Graves, one of Mark's closest friends, slashed Lemieux, breaking the Penguins center's left hand. Messier also missed Game 3, a 6-5 victory in overtime, and then Graves was suspended for four games the day before Game 4.

It marked a turning point in the series. With the hard-working, aggressive Graves sidelined— and with Messier not healthy—the loss of Lemieux would not hurt Pittsburgh too badly.

The Rangers were feeling down about the suspension and all the attention it drew. "Adam's a good kid who plays hard, but not dirty," Messier said. "Now, people think he's a dirty player. That's not fair."

Messier returned for Game 4, which the Rangers led 4-2 midway through the third period. But Ron Francis, who took over Lemieux's spot on Pittsburgh's top line, sent a long slapshot that fooled goalie Mike Richter, making it 4-3. The Rangers seemed to deflate and the Penguins became unstoppable. They tied it less than two minutes later, Francis scored in overtime, and suddenly, New York had lost its edge.

Pittsburgh won the fifth game, 3-2, at the Garden. The Penguins then routed the Rangers 5-1 to end the series—and keep the Cup-less streak going.

"I think the strike threw us off," coach Roger Neilson said. "The layoff seemed to help some teams, and hurt others."

"We couldn't overcome the controversy," Smith said. "We had the image of a goon squad." And the image of losers, as well.

"We've come a long way from October, but we still have a long way to go," Messier said. "Sometimes you have the bitterness of defeat before you get the sweetness of victory. This is a very bitter pill now."

The pain didn't ease much when Messier became the first Ranger since Andy Bathgate in 1959 to be named league MVP. "It's important to me that I came here with the idea that I had to establish myself in everyone's eyes with what I could do here in this dressing room and on the ice here," Mark said. "I felt right from the get-go that I couldn't rest on my laurels with what I had done in Edmonton and still earn their respect here.

"I think that coming here, I have to earn it, and go through the battles and the wars with the players. That's where you really get the strong feeling for one another."

BUILDING TOWARD THE CUP

Before the New York Rangers would storm to the Stanley Cup, they had to survive the storm of 1992-93.

Coming off a superb regular season in which they had the most points in the NHL, the Rangers were among the favorites to win the championship entering Messier's second season in New York. They'd had bad luck (the players' strike) and bad health (Messier's back problems) the previous spring. Then one of their best players, Adam Graves, had made a bad mistake, slashing and breaking the hand of Pittsburgh superstar Mario Lemieux. In the end, the Rangers' string of bad endings continued. No Cup since 1940.

"There are times when you have to lose first before you win the Cup," Messier said. "That's the lesson we learned in Edmonton."

After a bright start in September 1992, the Rangers went into a deep slump. "I'm not sure

The 1994 playoffs between the Devils and Rangers featured a lot of hard hitting. Here Messier checks Tom Chorsky off the puck.

43

what's going on, but right now we're shuffling guys in and out of the lineup and we're not playing well, because we're not together as a team," Messier said. "It's just not sitting well with anybody. There's a lot of unsettlement on our team. . . . You don't have good feelings chemistry-wise coming from everyone."

The biggest problem was between the star player and the coach. Messier did not like Roger Neilson's style of moving players in and out of the lineup. He also felt the Rangers did not play enough hard-nosed hockey, the kind of game Messier excels at. He also felt that Neilson had been out-coached in the playoffs.

By early January, the Rangers were 16 points behind Pittsburgh. Some nights, they seemed to be going through the motions. So Neilson was fired, replaced by Ron Smith—even though Neilson just had received a contract extension in November. He blamed Messier. "Last year, Mark came in and gave us all hope for a Stanley Cup," Neilson said. "He was as good a leader as you can get on a hockey team. This year, he just didn't lead us. That was the difference as far as his contribution. I called a meeting with some of our key guys—Adam Graves, Mike Gartner, Kevin Lowe—and said, 'Mark just isn't leading us. You'll have to step in.'"

Messier denied Neilson's claim. "I don't think that's a fair statement at all. I think I have a great relationship with my teammates," he said. "I knew about the meeting. Obviously, that was one of the problems Roger and I had. Having a meeting like that behind my back didn't help. I'm captain of the team until someone takes it away from me."

Nobody was going to do that. But the Rangers weren't going to skate away with any championships that year, either. They struggled the rest of the season and didn't make the playoffs. It was, Messier admitted, one of the worst years of his career, even though he'd played in his 1,000th career game, made the All-Star game for the 11th season and led the Rangers with 66 assists and 91 points. "There's going to be enough points of view on what ought to be done from outside the organization," he said. "I think it's important for the organization itself to remain solid and let everybody else do the trashing."

Just after the season, Mike Keenan was hired as coach. Although Keenan had never won a

Messier scores his third goal of the third period against Martin Brodeur to give the Rangers a 3-3 tie, depriving the Devils of a chance to win the series on their home ice.

Stanley Cup with Philadelphia or Chicago, Messier approved of his hiring. "Mike works hard and he knows how to get the best out of people," Messier said.

One month into the 1993-94 season, the Rangers were near the top of the standings after signing forward Steve Larmer, defenseman Alex Karpovtsev, and goalie Glenn Healy. The stars were doing well, too. Goalie Mike Richter had a 20-game unbeaten streak. The All-Star Game, held in January at Madison Square Garden, featured four Rangers, and Richter was named the MVP.

Graves would set a team record with 52 goals. Gartner reached 600 goals for his career. Brian Leetch was the best defenseman in the league. And Messier was as dominant as ever. On January 31, 1994, Messier passed Hall of Fame center Alex Delvecchio to move into the top 10 in career points.

"A lot of players have gone through the National Hockey League," Messier said. "To be in a top 10 of all time is a great feeling. But it'll probably mean more when I'm finished. I still have a lot of hockey left."

The Rangers finished with the best record in the NHL. "They've got to be thinking they're going to the Stanley Cup," Pittsburgh defenseman Larry Murphy said.

The chase for the Cup began against the New York Islanders, who had haunted the Rangers for nearly 20 years. In 1975, their third year of life, the Islanders upset the Rangers in the first round of the playoffs, winning the deciding third game in overtime at the Garden. In 1980, the Islanders began a string of four straight Stanley Cups. It took them 11 years to do what the Rangers couldn't in 54: win a fourth NHL title.

Nowhere were the chants of "1-9-4-0" louder than at Nassau Coliseum. Islanders fans would never let Rangers fans forget how long it had been. But these Islanders were no longer a championship-quality team. The Rangers swept the series, winning by a combined 22 goals to three.

"Our plan was to attack the whole series, and we did," said Messier, who scored twice in the clincher. "We're a pretty good team when we attack."

"I'm picking them to go all the way," Islanders coach Al Arbour agreed.

Next up was pesky Washington, which had just eliminated heavily favored Pittsburgh in the first round. The Rangers just shrugged and won in five games. In the conference finals the Rangers faced another archrival, the Devils. The "Hudson River War" was how local newspapers described the series.

The opener was a classic. At the end of the second period, they were up 3-2. But with 42.7 seconds to go in regulation, Claude Lemieux tied it for New Jersey. Then came a bigger shock when, in the second overtime, Stephane Richer beat Richter. It was the Devils' first win over the Rangers, who had won all six games during the season.

The Rangers didn't want to go across the river to the Meadowlands down two games. "We knew we didn't play our best game, but we still were 42 seconds away from winning," Messier said.

Mark scored the winning goal in the first two minutes of an almost-perfect 4-0 win in Game 2. They weren't quite as good in the third game, and the Devils were a lot better. Once again, that meant double overtime. But this time, it was New York that won as Stephane Matteau—a little known defenseman—became an unlikely hero as he scored on a backhander.

Not surprisingly, the gutsy Devils came right back, winning 3-1 in Game 4, when Keenan outsmarted himself. The Rangers managed only 22 shots at Martin Brodeur, who was superb in front of the Devils' net. In fact, Keenan benched Richter after he allowed two first-period goals, then he sat out Leetch and other regulars for much of the action.

Keenan claimed the players were hurt. Those players said, "No way."

Messier didn't like what the coach had done, and he met with several players before the fifth game. It didn't help: the Rangers were flat, playing their worst game of the playoffs and losing at home 4-1.

They were on the brink of elimination, and no Rangers team had ever won a series it trailed 3-2. Messier, however, was unintimidated, and made his famous guarantee.

Messier's greatest game pushed the series to a deciding contest at the Garden. For three full periods, the teams used every ounce of energy, then found more to give. After Leetch beat Brodeur to make it 1-0, you could almost feel the building shake. The cheering continued right into the dying seconds of the third period.

When Brodeur went to the bench, giving the Devils a sixth attacker, the Rangers saw an empty net at the other end of the ice. "Put the puck in there and head to the finals," Messier thought.

With the fans beginning to count down the final seconds, New Jersey's Valeri Zelepukin took a shot in front. It was blocked. He got the rebound and shot. This one went in. The clock read 7.7.

The Garden went silent.

"It was tough after the third period," Leetch said. "But we regrouped in the locker room. Mark kept everyone up and said, 'We'll play all night if we have to, we'll win this game.'"

Through one overtime, neither team could win it. So, for the third time in the series, they went into a second overtime.

And it wasn't one of the stars who ended it. It was Matteau, the man who won Game 3, would be a hero again. Matteau carried the puck behind the New Jersey net and sent it in front. The puck went off the stick of sliding Devils defenseman Viacheslav Fetisov and past Brodeur.

The fans, as exhausted from watching as the players were from skating, had enough left to let out a long, loud cheer. The Rangers mobbed Matteau and hugged each other, relieved that such a tough, tight series was theirs, and that the chase for the Stanley Cup was alive. "I couldn't believe it," Matteau said. "I realized what happened in Game 3. I still don't believe what happened in Game 7."

"You just go numb," Devils forward Bill Guerin said. "It seems like the goal line is a yard thick and it takes the puck a long time to go over it, but it does. It's not a good feeling. I wouldn't wish it on anybody."

The Rangers certainly wished it had been easier against the Devils. But they also knew what they'd done was special. But there was still another series to go, against Vancouver.

"This was a big step, a huge step," Messier said. "But our goal wasn't to make the playoffs. Our goal wasn't to get to the third round. Our goal wasn't to get to the Stanley Cup finals. Our goal is to win the Cup."

THE CUP COMES TO NEW YORK

The Rangers were in the Stanley Cup finals for the first time since 1979. But it wasn't anything new for Messier, Adam Graves, Kevin Lowe, Esa Tikkanen, Glenn Anderson, and Steve Larmer, who all had finals experience.

Nobody would lead more than Messier. "You can ask any guy here and they will say he's a different guy than they've ever played with," said Graves, who won a Stanley Cup with the Edmonton Oilers—and Messier—in 1990. "He's very upbeat, very positive. He doesn't get down on people. He's much more likely to praise someone for doing something right than criticize them for doing something wrong."

The Rangers were confident as they got ready for the surprising Vancouver Canucks. "When your best player is as hard a worker as Mess is—and we can all see him doing whatever it takes to

The Rangers hadn't won a Stanley Cup since 1940 —but Messier helped that losing streak come to an end in the finals against the Vancouver Canucks in 1994.

51

win—guys really have no choice but to follow him," Brian Leetch said. "Just his presence gives you that confidence, makes everybody do what they do best. If he's going to go all out, we'll do it, too."

Vancouver, with explosive scorer Pavel Bure and stingy goaltender Kirk McLean, had players who worked every bit as hard as Messier and the Rangers.

It was almost scary how alike the first game of the semifinals and the finals were. The Rangers dominated, but were held off by McLean, who made 52 saves. Still, New York was able to get two shots past him and led 2-1 heading into the final minute.

But goalie Mike Richter made a mistake on a shot by Sergio Momesso and Martin Gelinas poked the rebound off Richter's left arm. It dribbled into the net, forcing overtime. It was the third time in eight games that the Rangers had blown a lead late in the third period. "Things like that are going to happen and there's not a thing you can do about them," Messier said. "So it's not about what happens to you, it's how you react to it."

The Rangers reacted by sending 14 shots on McLean in the first eight and a half minutes of the extra period. McLean stopped them all. With 40 seconds left in the first overtime, Leetch's slapshot hit the crossbar. It rebounded to the Canucks, who headed the other way. Greg Adams's slapper beat Richter with 33.1 seconds remaining.

"Maybe we stole one, thanks to McLean," Vancouver coach Pat Quinn said.

Just as against New Jersey, the Rangers were desperate in the second game, not wanting to go on the road down 0-2. Messier made a big play, stealing the puck and setting up longtime line-mate Anderson for the go-ahead goal in a 3-1 victory that evened the series. "We've played together long enough to know that he would be right on my tail," said Messier. "I knew once the puck went by the net, if it somehow got in front, he'd find a way."

Said Anderson: "Playing with a great player such as Messier, he definitely tends to bring your game up another level."

The Rangers would stay at that level in Van-couver, sweeping both games to bring home a 3-1 lead.

Bure was thrown out of Game 3 for high-stick-ing Jay Wells in the face late in the first period. The score was 1-1 when it happened, and the Rangers scored the next four goals.

"What did losing Pavel mean? Try taking Mark Messier away from them," Vancouver's Gerald Diduck said.

Bure was back for the fourth game. In the sec-ond period, with Vancouver ahead 2-1, Bure was awarded a penalty shot. The NHL's leading goal-scorer in both the regular season (60) and play-offs (14) is considered the league's best on break-aways. But Richter forced Bure to make a move and then made a right leg save. "He came out from the net and that's why I couldn't shoot," Bure said. "He backed up right away. I tried to fake him, but he didn't give me any room."

Sergei Zubov tied the score late in the period, then Leetch set up Alexei Kovalev's winner in a 4-2 victory. Leetch had a goal and three assists. So it was back home to the Garden to wrap it up.

"Right now is not a time to be looking too far ahead," Messier warned. "We're not going to fall into that trap."

Messier shows off the Stanley Cup to a rejoicing crowd during a ticker-tape parade down New York City's Broadway.

With parade routes already mapped out and Stanley Cup ceremonies planned—including hats reading "Stanley Cup Champion New York Rangers"—the Rangers forgot one important item: winning. In one of the wildest games the finals has seen, the Canucks took a 3-0 lead in the third period. Maybe they began thinking about the series going back to Vancouver, because New York scored three goals in 3:33 to knot the score. Doug Lidster, Steve Larmer and—who else?—Messier scored.

At that point, did anyone believe the Rangers weren't going to skate right over the Canucks on their way to picking up the Cup? Apparently Vancouver's players didn't believe it. Just as the Garden had come to life, it quickly went silent. The chants of "We Want the Cup" stopped as Dave Babych, Geoff Courtnall, and Bure scored. Vancouver won 6-3.

"From experience, this is the toughest game to win," Messier said. "It's a tough loss, but we learned a lot, that the clinching game of anything is always tough, and we found that out tonight."

They would find it out again in Game 6, back in Vancouver. The Canucks had never won the

Cup since their birth in 1970 and had been in the finals only one other time, losing to the Islanders in 1982. The city of Vancouver and the whole west coast of Canada were ready for a celebration, just as New York was.

As their fans waved towels and chanted "Go Canucks Go," the team did just that, sending the series back to New York with a 4-1 victory. "We were either going golfing or getting back on a plane, and we're getting back on a plane," Diduck said.

"We don't have anything to hang our heads about," Messier said. "We have the opportunity to go home and win the Stanley Cup."

The Rangers hadn't won any of their previous three Cups at home. They hadn't won the NHL championship since 1940. Was that sad history now haunting them heading into Game 7?

"About that jinx or curse, I don't think that really matters," Vancouver's Babych said. "They have a lot of experience. They have Mark Messier and guys who know how to win and they're going to come out the next game and try to put all the guns to us."

Leetch opened the scoring and Graves made it 2-0. But this team did nothing easily, and Vancouver's Trevor Linden made it 2-1 with a short-handed goal in the second period.

The Rangers responded. Naturally, it was Messier who led them.

He scored on a power play later in the middle period. "The big goal was Messier's," said Linden, who would get the Canucks' second goal, making it 3-2 with 15½ minutes to go.

Rangers' fans had their hearts in their throats. They could not forget how the Rangers had failed to protect leads like this three times in the playoffs.

"That's when you turn to your leaders," Keenan said. "That's when the players you brought in to lead your team, players like Mark, take over."

Messier checked like crazy, playing double shifts and winning every important face-off. Richter made some great saves and was helped when Nathan Lafayette's shot hit the goal post. Leetch was everywhere.

The fans were on their feet for nearly the entire third period. In the final moments, there couldn't have been any food sold in the stands—everyone was too busy biting fingernails or holding hands and praying. That's what 54 years without a championship can do.

"We were excited, too, as it got closer to the end," Messier said. "But on the bench, I could tell we were calm enough. We were thinking about doing our jobs and if each guy did his job, we could win."

Messier won a final face-off with 1.6 seconds to go. The clock turned to 0:00. The drought was over. No more "1-9-4-0" chants in enemy arenas. No more jokes about 54 years without being No. 1. "Now I Can Die in Peace" read a sign in the stands.

The Stanley Cup had been delivered to New York, and Mark Messier was the main reason. Messier shook with happiness as he grabbed the Stanley Cup trophy and held it high. At that moment, Messier was king of the hockey world for the sixth time, king of New York for the first.

"The attention that was paid to the game was incredible," Messier said. "It's just great for the game of hockey. I've never seen anything like it, and I've been in the game for 16 years. I've won five Stanley Cups before this and I've never experienced anything like it the last two months. I thought I'd seen it all and I really wasn't saying much, but in my own mind I was saying, 'This is absolutely incredible.'"

So was the ticker-tape parade down Broadway, attended by about 1.5 million people. Messier brought the Cup onstage at "The Late Show with David Letterman." His teammates would spend the entire summer showing it off at home—and that meant all over the United States and Canada and even in Europe.

"We're going to celebrate this like we've never celebrated anything in our lives," Messier concluded. "Once you get a taste of the Cup, you never want to lose it."

Bringing the Stanley Cup to New York made Messier as big a hero as anyone in the Big Apple. His face was plastered all over billboards and magazine covers. He made dozens of commercials.

Called the most eligible bachelor in the metropolitan area, he was seen with Madonna and famous models. He was a regular on the major TV talk shows. Just as he'd conquered Edmonton years before, Messier was the King of New York in 1994.

He did other things to earn that title. His work with charities such as Tomorrows Children's Fund, to which he donated money for every goal he scored, has been special to Mark. "I have seen these kids who have life-threatening diseases or problems they have to battle, and I realize how lucky I am to be able to do what I do and to be healthy," he said. "Anything I can do for them is what I want to do."

Through the Mark Messier Point Club and Messier's own foundation, nearly $500,000 has been raised for Tomorrows Children's Fund. Mark also conducted clinics for inner city youths

Messier has donated time and money to numerous charitable events. Here he makes an appearance with Cindy Crawford during a fundraiser for DISHES (Determined Involved Supermodels Helping to End Suffering).

in the New York area, trying to spread the popularity of his sport.

On the ice, he continues to be a force. While the Rangers have struggled since winning the championship—Mike Keenan quit as coach soon after the Cup was won; a half-season lockout ruined 1994-95; injuries to key players, including Messier, have slowed the team—there still was strong hope Messier would get a seventh Stanley Cup ring. Especially since in 1996, Wayne Gretzky joined the Rangers.

When the Rangers had the chance to sign hockey's greatest all-time scorer as a free agent last summer, the team's general manager, Neil Smith, had a talk with Messier. "Over the years, Mark and I chatted about all the guys he played with," Smith says. "Mark had mentioned several times to do everything I could to get Wayne if I saw the chance."

"This is the greatest player in hockey, someone who could add 110, 120, 130, or even 140 points to our team," Messier says. "Every team Wayne has been on, he's made better. He makes the players around him better. He gets the fans interested. And when you give him the support, Wayne wins."

Messier defended Gretzky from people who said he had aged. "He won't score 215 points anymore, but he will elevate our players to a different level. I've never played with anybody else of Wayne's ability."

Nobody was more excited about rejoining Messier than Gretzky, even if both were in the final stage of their careers at age 36. "I'm probably the only free agent to come to New York for less money," Gretzky joked. "What tipped the scales was to play with Mark and with a team focused on winning a championship.

"Mark has won more Cups than anyone else playing in the league," he added. "He's the best leader in the game. He was a hidden jewel in Edmonton, because I overshadowed him, but he was such a team player, the most unselfish player I've played with. It rubbed off on the whole team. When I came to New York, I understood this was Mark's team, and that's the way it should be. Look at all he did for New York. My responsibility is to take some of the burden off Mark."

The focus wasn't just on the ice for the buddies. Mark and Wayne held the main roles in one of Fox Television's ads for its NHL telecasts. Gretzky played neat Felix Unger to Messier's messy Oscar Madison in a hockey version of the popular "Odd Couple." For a scene in which Felix spears Oscar's cigar butt with his umbrella on the TV show, Messier threw down an apple core and Gretzky used a hockey stick to flip it into a garbage can.

In 1997, the Rangers had only a decent season, but they started to play better during the playoffs. In the second round, they defeated the favored Devils, as Messier and Gretzky each had a terrific series. But Philadelphia put an end to the Rangers' Stanley Cup dreams as big Eric Lindros could not be stopped.

It was the fond dream of numerous Ranger fans that Messier and Gretzky would retire together after bringing another Stanley Cup to New York. They pictured the two skating off on their way to the Hall of Fame after celebrating one more night of glory on the ice.

It wouldn't happen. At the end of the 1997 season, Messier's contract was up and while the Rangers made him a strong offer, the Vancouver Canucks made him an even stronger one. They put a three-year, $20-million deal on the table and Messier accepted.

Vancouver hopes that Messier will bring the winning attitude he has carried with him all his career. Messier himself pointed out that the team had almost gone all the way in 1994—after all, it was his Rangers that had denied them the championship that year.

STATISTICS

MARK MESSIER

Season	Team	League	Regular Season				Playoffs			
			GP	G	A	P	GP	G	A	P
1977-78	Port	WHL	0	0	0	0	7	4	1	5
1978-79	Indi/ Cinc	WHA	52	1	10	11	0	0	0	0
1979-80	Edmo	NHL	75	12	21	33	3	1	2	3
1980-81	Edmo	NHL	72	23	40	63	9	2	5	7
1981-82	Edmo	NHL	78	50	38	88	5	1	2	3
1982-83	Edmo	NHL	77	48	58	106	15	15	6	21
1983-84	Edmo	NHL	73	37	64	101	19	8	18	26
1984-85	Edmo	NHL	55	23	31	54	18	12	13	25
1985-86	Edmo	NHL	63	35	49	84	10	4	6	10
1986-87	Edmo	NHL	77	37	70	107	21	12	16	28
1987-88	Edmo	NHL	77	37	74	111	19	11	23	34
1988-89	Edmo	NHL	72	33	61	94	7	1	11	12
1989-90	Edmo	NHL	79	45	84	129	22	9	22	31
1990-91	Edmo	NHL	53	12	51	63	18	4	11	15
1991-92	NYR	NHL	79	35	72	107	11	7	7	14
1992-93	NYR	NHL	75	25	66	91	0	0	0	0
1993-94	NYR	NHL	76	26	58	84	23	12	18	30
1994-95	NYR	NHL	46	14	39	53	10	3	10	13
1995-96	NYR	NHL	74	47	52	99	11	4	7	11
1996-97	NYR	NHL	71	36	48	84	15	3	9	12
Totals			1324	576	986	1562	243	113	187	300

GP   games played
G   goals
A   assists
PTS   points

MARK DOUGLAS MESSIER
A CHRONOLOGY

1961 Born on January 18 in Edmonton, Alberta.

1977 Picked in the third round of the NHL draft, number 48 overall.

1979 Joins Wayne Gretzky as a member of the Edmonton Oilers.

1983 Scores over 100 points for the first time and is named to the All-Star team.

1984 Leads Oilers to their best season and first Stanley Cup championship; is named playoff MVP.

1985 Helps Oilers achieve back-to-back championships.

1987 Leads Oilers to their third Stanley Cup title.

1988 Helps Oilers become a dynasty with their second back-to-back championship.

1990 Now the captain of the Oilers, as Gretzky has been traded, Messier again leads Edmonton to a championship—his fifth.

1991 Joins New York Rangers.

1994 Leads Rangers to their first Stanley Cup championship in 54 years.

1997 Signs three-year deal with Vancouver Canucks.

SUGGESTIONS FOR FURTHER READING

Farber, Michael. "Mano a Mano." *Sports Illustrated*, May 13, 1996.

Martin, Deirdre. "Mark Messier and Me." *Seventeen*, December, 1995.

Montville, Leigh. "Sudden Impact." *Sports Illustrated*, March 16, 1992.

Murphy, Austin, "The Look of a Winner." *Sports Illustrated*, May 9, 1988.

Swift, E. M. "The Good Old Days." *Sports Illustrated*, October 7, 1996.

ABOUT THE AUTHOR

Barry Wilner has been a sportswriter for the Associated Press for 20 years. In that time, he has covered the Super Bowl, Olympics, World Cup, Stanley Cup finals, and many other sporting events. He has written books on hockey, soccer, swimming, and Olympic sports. He is the author of *Dan Marino* in Chelsea House's Football Legends series, *Reggie Miller* in the Basketball Legends series, plus books about today's golf stars in the Female Superstars and Male Superstars series. He lives in Garnerville, NY, with his wife, Helene, daughters Nicole, Jamie, and Tricia, and son Evan.

INDEX